Gnosticism

N. R. NEEDHAM

Copyright © The Christian Institute 2022

The author has asserted his right under Section 77 of the Copyright, Designs & Patents Act 1988 to be identified as the author of this work.

Printed in December 2022

ISBN 978-1-901086-64-5

Published by:
The Christian Institute, Wilberforce House, 4 Park Road, Gosforth Business Park, Newcastle upon Tyne, NE12 8DG

All rights reserved

No part of this publication may be reproduced, or stored in a retrieval system, or transmitted, in any form or by any means, mechanical, electronic, photocopying, recording or otherwise, without the prior permission of The Christian Institute.

All scripture quotations, unless otherwise indicated, are taken from The ESV® Bible (The Holy Bible, English Standard Version®), copyright © 2001 by Crossway, a publishing ministry of Good News Publishers. Used by permission. All rights reserved.

The Christian Institute is a Company Limited by Guarantee, registered in England as a charity. Company No. 263 4440, Charity No. 100 4774. A charity registered in Scotland. Charity No. SC039220

Contents

5   Introduction

7   The biblical setting

13   Gnosticism: background

17   The Gnostic rejection of creation

21   Gnostic sexuality

29   Conclusion

31   Appendix: The enduring significance of gender

35   References

Introduction

The Western world, it hardly needs saying, has undergone a massive self-acknowledged revolution since the 1960s in its attitudes to human sexual ethics. It began with Hippie-style "free love": the rejection of the allegedly moribund and constricting institution of marriage as the proper context for sexual activity. Then it went on to encompass homosexuality and lesbianism, and then the political redefinition of marriage (to include man plus man, and woman plus woman). Now it embraces transgenderism – in which biological males feel that they are inwardly female, and biological females that they are inwardly male, and may consequently undergo chemical and surgical treatment in an attempt to conform their biology to their sense of self.

What is perhaps not quite so widely recognised is that almost all of the above, one way or another, has its counterpart in an ancient spiritual movement known as Gnosticism, which flourished in the second and third centuries. This is not necessarily to say that any of those promoting the modern agenda are self-consciously Gnostics. Yet the analogy between Gnostic beliefs and modern attitudes is striking, as we shall see. Moreover, the Gnostics of old tried to convince Christians and Pagans alike that *they*, the Gnostics, were the genuine Christians.

This meant that the early Church felt it was duty-bound to engage in a controversy of ideas with Gnosticism, in order to challenge this confusing claim. Some indeed in the modern era have explicitly reproduced the claim that Gnosticism was (and is) true Christianity. At a popular level, for example, John Lennon of the Beatles once put it like this: "the only true Christians were the Gnostics who believe in self-knowledge, i.e. becoming Christ themselves, reaching the Christ within."[1]

We shall, in a moment, consider how the ancient Gnostic movement contained virtually all of the modern sexual agenda, albeit ancient Gnosticism often held this only in an intensely religious (i.e. non-secular) form. Consequently it would be true to say, as so very often in Church history and its controversies of belief and ideas, that (in the words of the Preacher in the book of Ecclesiastes) "there is nothing new under the sun":

> "What has been is what will be, and what has been done is what will be done, and there is nothing new under the sun. Is there a thing of which it is said, 'See, this is new'? It has been already in the ages before us" (Ecclesiastes 1:9-10).

First of all, however, let us begin by considering the biblical backdrop to the values of the early Church. This will help us to see what inspired that foundational generation of Christians to argue that Gnostic ideas and authentically Christian ideas were two different things.

The biblical setting

In the narrative of the Bible, as that narrative has been read and understood by the vast majority of its readers (including those who disagree with it, but read it without Gnostic assumptions), what we might call 'gender norms' are established by God the Creator, in the creation account given in Genesis chapters 1 and 2. Chapter 1 describes the creation of humanity in such a way that the distinction between male and female is built into the centre of the account:

> "So God created man in his own image, in the image of God he created him; male and female he created them" (Genesis 1:27).

'Male and female' involves, among other things, the capacity for sexual reproduction when the two are united:

> "God blessed them. And God said to them, 'Be fruitful and multiply and fill the earth and subdue it'" (Genesis 1:28).

The divine differentiation of humanity into male and female is such that it enables those first humans to reproduce – to be fruitful, increase in number, and fill the earth. In other words, the Genesis narrative is speaking of biological maleness and femaleness with their capacity, when united, to beget more humans.

The same understanding is found in the second creation account of Genesis 2. This account differs from Genesis 1 in focusing more intently on the human race, rather than on the world in general.

In this account, Adam (which means simply "Man" or "The Man" in Hebrew) is fashioned by the Creator from the soil of the earth (v.7). However, the Man is at first "alone", that is, without the companionship of Woman. God pronounces this aloneness of Adam "not good" (v.18, the only thing in the pre-Fall creation deemed not to be good). To remedy the deficiency, God fashions the Woman, Eve, from the Man's side (vv.21-22). So there emerges the Woman as the true companion of the Man, and the Man of the Woman: a companionship not only spiritual but physical in nature. The emphasis on the Woman's physical derivation from the Man shows that the material, biological differentiation between the two is integral to the Creator's purpose. Man precisely as Man, and Woman precisely as Woman, made and intended for each other in their maleness and femaleness, stand forth in the Genesis account.[2]

Adam and Eve are then immediately presented as the model or prototype of man-woman marriage:

> "Then the man said, 'This at last is bone of my bones and flesh of my flesh; she shall be called Woman, because she was taken out of Man'. Therefore a man shall leave his father and his mother and hold fast to his wife, and they shall become one flesh" (Genesis 2:23-24).

Marriage between Man, created as Man, and Woman, created as Woman, is the fundamental form of human companionship in Genesis, existing in Eden prior to the Fall.

In Genesis chapter 3, this is all underlined afresh in what God says concerning the Woman. First, it is she to whom the function of child-bearing is assigned:

> "To the woman he said, 'I will surely multiply your pain in childbearing; in pain you shall bring forth children'" (Genesis 3:16).

Whatever "Woman" means according to the Creator's design, Genesis indicates that it involves the capacity for childbearing.

Then, if we go forward to Genesis 3:20, the reason for the Woman's name "Eve" is given. "Eve" is Hebrew for 'life'. The text says:

> "The Man called his wife's name Eve, because she was the mother of all living."

The Woman is to be the biological mother of all the descendants of the original couple. Once again, the Genesis account of human identity includes the traditional biological relationships with which we are familiar. Man is husband to the Woman, and thence father: Woman is wife to the Man, and thence mother. No doubt Man and Woman are *more* than this, but they are not *other* than this. Biblically, the only alternative is the special divine calling of singleness for the sake of the Kingdom, exemplified supremely in the sacrificial service of Jesus himself and (in imitation of Jesus) the apostle Paul (see Matthew 19:10-12, 1 Corinthians 7:7, 27).

It almost goes without saying: the Genesis narrative does not offer any hint that this original God-created design of biological maleness and femaleness had anything wrong, artificial, subjective, or malleable about it. It is simply the 'creation ordinance' of human existence and human gender, established by a good, wise God for his human offspring.[3]

This view of Man and Woman, embedded in the creation accounts of early Genesis, is then reflected in the New Testament. In the Gospels of Matthew and Mark, the writers record Jesus as referring back to the opening of the book of Genesis for his own understanding of marriage. In Mark's Gospel, Jesus is recorded as saying:

> "From the beginning of creation, 'God made them male and female.' 'Therefore a man shall leave his father and mother and hold fast to his wife, and the two shall become one flesh.' So they are no longer two but one flesh. What therefore God has joined together, let not man separate." (Mark 10:6-9)[4]

In other words, Jesus does not establish a new ordinance of marriage for the people of the New Covenant, but re-establishes its original form attested in Genesis 1-2. Marriage is between a man and a woman; these male and female identities include biology, since the two are to become "one flesh", a biblical way of indicating the physical union in marriage from which God intends children to be born. Even the Man who marries is himself described as a child of a "father and mother".

Virtually the whole of biblical sexual ethics, Old and New Testament alike, is rooted in the account of primal human existence testified in Genesis 1-3, and Jesus' reinforcement of this in Mark 10 (and its parallel in Matthew 19). The celebration of marriage, fidelity in marriage, the rearing of children, the sin of adultery, the possibility of divorce or separation, the possibility of remarriage after divorce (at least in some Christian traditions), the aberration of non-heterosexual lifestyles, and the special calling of singleness all flow from this original fountain in the outlook of the Bible. "From the beginning of creation, 'God made them male and female'."

It should also be noted that if we take Jesus himself as the ultimate norm of human life, he too – in a higher and more perfect sense – exists in a marriage relationship. He is the divine-human Bridegroom, and the Church (all who are united with him through faith) is his Bride. The apostle Paul speaks extensively of this in Ephesians 5:22-33. The heart of this passage reads:

> "Husbands, love your wives, as Christ loved the church and gave himself up for her, that he might sanctify her, having cleansed her by the washing of water with the

> word, so that he might present the church to himself in splendour, without spot or wrinkle or any such thing, that she might be holy and without blemish. In the same way husbands should love their wives as their own bodies. He who loves his wife loves himself. For no one ever hated his own flesh, but nourishes and cherishes it, just as Christ does the church, because we are members of his body. 'Therefore a man shall leave his father and mother and hold fast to his wife, and the two shall become one flesh.' This mystery is profound, and I am saying that it refers to Christ and the church."[5]
> (Ephesians 5:25-33)

For the apostle Paul, human marriage on the earthy, biological level, bears witness to this glorious Christological reality. Remove the biological scaffolding, however, and everything to which it testifies Christologically becomes devoid of reference and meaning.

From this biblical backdrop of understanding, which moulded the thinking of the early Church, let us now look at the Gnostic movement with which early Christianity found itself enmeshed in so deep a controversy of ideas, including ideas about gender.

Gnosticism: background

Gnosticism was the first great crisis of thought and self-definition to strike the early Church after the apostles. The crisis endured throughout the second and third centuries. Indeed, the most daunting task facing the early Church fathers was simply to distinguish between Christianity and Gnosticism, for the benefit both of fellow Christians and of Pagan inquirers. This was because Gnostics (as noted previously) claimed that they were the true Christians; and they enjoyed remarkable success in convincing multitudes of this claim. Gnostic sects expanded astronomically across the face of the Roman Empire, with an astonishing variety of names – Barbelonites, Cainites, Cerinthians, Encratites, Justinians, Marcionites, Marcosians, Nicolaitans, Ophites, Sethians, Severians, and Valentinians, to name a few.

The common name for these groups, 'Gnostic', derives from the Greek word *gnosis*, 'knowledge'. In spite of the differences between the various Gnostic sects, they generally claimed to possess a knowledge that had been taught privately by Jesus to the apostles, and passed on secretly to the initiated few; this knowledge, essential to human salvation, was (they said) unavailable to the general mass of Christians through their teachers or their scriptures. It was impossible, Gnostics argued, to understand the Gospel correctly without this secret knowledge, and the various Gnostic sects had their own Scriptures containing their version of the gnosis. The most famous Gnostic scripture is the *Gospel of Thomas*; it was probably written in Syria sometime in the second century AD, and records over a hundred alleged sayings of Jesus.

In many ways, the Gnostic vision of Christianity clashed very deeply and fundamentally with the Gospel taught in all those churches which had either been founded by the apostles, or where the apostles were known to have ministered. The basic teaching of those churches was summed up in the Apostles' Creed, with which historic Christianity has always identified up to the present day.[6]

One of the most definitional Gnostic beliefs, setting Gnosticism apart from apostolic Christianity, was the Gnostic contempt for 'flesh', physical matter. Perhaps influenced by prominent strains in Greek philosophy, Gnostics posited a total antithesis between spirit and flesh (some of us today might perhaps say 'mind and matter'). These are so alien to each other, Gnostics said, and spirit is so superior in nature, that flesh is the absolute enemy of spirit. Consequently, since God is the supremely and perfectly spiritual being, he by definition can have no contact with the inferior world of flesh. This of course involved a denial that God had created the world of physical matter; its creator, according to Gnosticism, was a lesser being whom they called "the Demiurge" (Greek for 'architect'). This Demiurge-creator of matter and flesh was a foolish, bungling entity who had created a vile and repulsive universe. The human spirit was a divine spark trapped within an alien body of flesh; liberation and escape from the tyranny of the fleshly body constituted the Gnostic idea of salvation.

We may be able to see the beginnings of this flesh-rejecting Gnosticism recorded in the New Testament itself, most notably in the First Epistle of John:

> "By this you know the Spirit of God: every spirit that confesses that Jesus Christ has come in the flesh is from God, and every spirit that does not confess Jesus is not from God" (1 John 4:2-3).

John's caution against a Christianity which denied that the Redeemer has "come in the flesh" may well be John's warning against an early form of Gnosticism.

This Gnostic animus against the flesh led not only to an

unbiblical denigration and loathing of human flesh (in contrast to the biblical affirmation in Psalm 139:14 that the human body is "fearfully and wonderfully made"). Even more significantly, it also led to a rejection of the fundamental Christian belief in the Incarnation, that is, God becoming flesh to save people of flesh (such as all humans are). As noted above, John seems to be warning against such a denial of the Incarnation in 1 John 4. It also clashes with John's positive teaching in his Gospel:

> "In the beginning was the Word, and the Word was with God, and the Word was God… And the Word became flesh and dwelt among us" (John 1:1, 14).

Gnosticism disbelieved this claim about the divine Word becoming human flesh. How could the heavenly Redeemer, in all his pure spirituality of nature, possibly have become crude flesh? Jesus, therefore, according to Gnostics, only *seemed* to have a fleshly body; but in reality he was a non-physical spirit-being. From this consideration, Gnosticism became known as *docetic* (from the Greek "to seem" – Jesus only seemed to be a man of flesh). A discerning mind will already see how, from such Gnostic rejection of flesh and exaltation of spirit, a line can be drawn to the modern view of the human self. This view is, in essence, that the self is an autonomous psychological entity, unconstrained by its biology (flesh), and therefore able to declare itself as any gender.

We have two chief sources for our knowledge of Gnosticism:

(i) The writings of the early Church fathers, especially Irenaeus of Lyons (active AD 175-195). Irenaeus' masterpiece was his *Against Heresies*, a five-volume work in which Irenaeus sets out to refute the Gnostic claim that Gnosticism is genuine apostolic Christianity. Because Irenaeus describes in some detail the Gnostic systems he is refuting, his work is a goldmine of information about Gnostic beliefs. Another important source is the *Refutation of All Heresies* by the early Church father Hippolytus (died AD 236).

(ii) Until recently, we were totally dependent on what the early Church fathers said for our knowledge of Gnosticism. However, in 1945 a large earthenware jar was discovered at Nag Hammadi in Egypt, buried on a mountain, containing an important collection of ancient Gnostic documents. These Nag Hammadi documents (not to be confused with the Dead Sea Scrolls) have now been translated into English, and they enable us to see from the Gnostics' own writings what they believed.

The two modern scholars who have probably done most to popularise Gnosticism from the Nag Hammadi documents are Elaine Pagels and James Robinson. Elaine Pagels (born 1943) has a PhD from Harvard University; she is a respected and award-winning academic, who has used her position as Harrington Spear Paine Professor of Religion at Princeton to teach and disseminate her views. Pagels introduced the Gnostics to a new audience in 1979 in her highly influential book *The Gnostic Gospels*. In this work, she presents the Gnostics as the heralds of true enlightened Christianity, and the early Church fathers as narrow-minded, heresy-hunting persecutors, who invented the myth of Satan to demonise their opponents. She elaborated on this in other significant works such as *The Gnostic Paul* and *Adam, Eve and the Serpent*.

James Robinson (1924-2016) was director of the Institute for Antiquity and Christianity, and the scholar who headed up the translation of the Nag Hammadi documents into English. In his introduction to the English version of the Nag Hammadi documents, Robinson showed himself sympathetic to the Gnostics, and joined with Elaine Pagels in condemning the early Church fathers as narrow-minded heresy-hunters.

The Gnostic rejection of creation

We do not have time to explore further all the distinctives of the Gnostics. However, we do wish to examine those areas of belief in which some or all Gnostics were involved in a clash of ideas with the teaching of the early Church, where that teaching was itself grounded in Genesis 1-3 and its reaffirmation by Jesus and Paul. The first main area where this is significant was the Gnostic rejection of creation and created norms. The Genesis account of creation, especially human creation, was disowned and radically reinterpreted in Gnosticism. This had profound implications for the understanding of gender.[7]

In its theory of creation, and indeed redemption (which is God's gracious act of re-creation), Gnosticism rejected the male-female balance found in the Genesis account. Animated by a negative evaluation of maleness, Gnosticism exalted the female over the male. This found vivid expression in the central figure in Gnostic mythology and spirituality, a female redeemer named Sophia (the Greek feminine word for wisdom). Gnosticism, we recollect, refused to identify the Old Testament Creator-God with the supreme God; the latter, for Gnostics, is essentially unrevealed and unknowable, but his cosmic ambassador is Sophia, the Mother of the universe.

Sophia's great mission in the Gnostic scheme is twofold: (i) to expose the wickedness of the Old Testament Creator-God Yahweh – he is a foolish male god, ignorant and arrogant, fit only to be mocked; (ii) to lead humanity out of its bondage to Yahweh, and bring it to the liberating Gnostic concept of spiritual truth. After death, Gnostics taught, Yahweh and his evil angels would try to bring the soul under their power; it was only by invoking Sophia that the soul could escape into the Gnostic heaven. Sophia's final destiny was to cast Yahweh into hell. In other words, to put it bluntly, Sophia's work was to bring an end to what was perceived to be the false, tyrannical, masculine God of the Bible.

The Gnostic interpretation of Creator, Man and Woman in Genesis 1-3 becomes extremely relevant at this point. According to Gnosticism, the God of Genesis – despite his pretensions to goodness – is evil, and the enemy of Adam and Eve. He tries to keep them in an oppressive state of ignorance, by jealously forbidding them to eat from the tree of knowledge. But help is at hand in the form of Sophia. She enters into the serpent, who then teaches true wisdom to Eve, encouraging her to break the cruel and despotic commands of Yahweh, and eat from the tree of knowledge. In the Gnostic reading of Genesis 3, the Sophia-possessed serpent thus becomes a liberator and redeemer. Eve listens to Sophia, and so becomes the heroine of the story, leading Adam to join her in rejecting the Creator-God and seizing upon true wisdom.

With such a backdrop to its understanding of the universe, it is little wonder that the created norms of male and female expounded in Genesis 1 and 2 had no value in Gnosticism. As we shall see in a moment, this played out in a way uncannily similar to what has taken place in Western culture today. Our modern experience can satirically yet accurately be described in the title of Peter Jones's book, *The Gnostic Empire Strikes Back*. Before, however, we come to the Gnostic denial of a Genesis-grounded understanding of male and female that has reawakened in our time, let us continue to survey the female-orientated, goddess-centred spirituality of Gnosticism, as this finds a voice in the New Age movement. In so many ways, this has provided the spiritual inspiration for the deconstruction of what Genesis says about the nature and roles of male and female.

The New Age movement, which has conquered the 'spirituality' section in so many bookshops, is at its heart a revived form of Gnosticism. Like its Gnostic roots, New Age spirituality is resoundingly feminine and goddess-worshipping. It rejects male images of God, especially the biblical revelation of God in Jesus Christ as "Father", a perception regarded as spiritually oppressive and destructive. In this respect, an important New Age feminist book was published in 1982, entitled *The Politics of Women's Spirituality*, with chapters by leading feminist thinkers like Mary Daly and Naomi Goldenberg. A glance at some of the chapter titles reveals: *Why Women Need the Goddess: Phenomenological, Psychological and Political Reflections*, *Witchcraft as Goddess Religion*, and *The Origins of Music: Women's Goddess Worship*. The whole book is a literary monument to the return of the goddess.[8]

Nor are New Agers pursuing a *secular* feminist agenda in this; the phenomenon is profoundly spiritual, guided by spiritual forces of which leading New Agers are often conscious. For example, through a New Age medium, a spirit-entity calling itself "Lazaris" channelled the following message about the glorious return of the goddess to Western civilisation: "Though She never left, the Goddess is returning to you... and She brings a Light... Yours is the Great Work: Receiving and then bringing Her Light into a seemingly darkening world. She is returning to you and She brings gifts and treasures that are bountiful and without limit... As She returns, you can come to know the Goddess and you can know God... you can come to know who you are."[9]

In New Age spirituality, the feminine principle is often acknowledged in the shape of Isis, the ancient Egyptian goddess. Feminist thinker Kathleen Alexander-Berghorn says: "Today women are rediscovering Isis, recognizing her in the images that have come to us and celebrating her continuing presence in our lives through the creation of new rituals and works of art inspired by the Goddess. Each of us can personally experience the healing presence of the Goddess within us. 'All women are Isis and Isis is all women'."[10]

New Age feminism and witchcraft are also very closely linked. A leading feminist, Miriam Starhawk, a Wiccan priestess, states her overriding preference for Eastern over Western forms of religion, because "in many ways their philosophies are very close to that of witchcraft".[11] Naomi Goldenberg, a leading Jewish feminist, became a practising witch in order to pursue her feminist ideals.

Perhaps the most visible and notorious manifestation of goddess worship in a Christian context took place in 1993, at the "RE-imagining Conference" in Minneapolis, attended by 2,000 Christian women from mainstream American Protestant churches. In the opening session, the liturgy stated: "It is time to state clearly and dream wildly about who we intend to be in the future through the power and guidance of the spirit of wisdom whom we name Sophia." The Gnostic goddess Sophia was the central figure in the supposedly Christian worship of the Conference. It reached its climax in a sort of alternative Lord's Supper, where instead of bread and wine, milk and honey were distributed, over which the blessing was pronounced, "Our maker Sophia, we are women in your image."[12]

On a similar wavelength, James Robinson, head of the translation team for the Nag Hammadi documents, proposed that we should re-imagine Jesus as the incarnation of Sophia, and see him not as "very God and very Man" (the traditional confession) but as "very Goddess and very Man".[13]

Gnostic sexuality

A strong strain of Gnostic thought posited the true ideal of gender as 'androgyny'. This Greek term (literally 'man-woman' or 'male-female') describes in Gnosticism a non-biological form of 'sexual' identity, in which the physical forms of maleness and femaleness have been transcended. The result is a new type of being, in whom the male and female are combined and synthesised into one. In other words, Gnostics rejected the fixed distinction between man and woman, male and female: a counter-narrative to the one found in Genesis 1 and 2.[14]

For Gnosticism, the biological identifiers of maleness and femaleness are false and oppressive, a consequence or even the cause of the Fall. In the Gnostic scheme, we remember, the God of Genesis who creates male and female is not even the true or supreme God, but a lesser entity whom they called "the Demiurge". This Demiurge-creator, however, since he is foolish and evil, has fashioned a bad creation; the physical world he has made, especially his separation of humanity into male and female, is an aspect of his repulsive handiwork from which we must seek to escape. The true self rejects the biological definitions imposed by the false Creator.

We find this rejection of the male-female distinction, and the alternative ideal of androgyny, clearly expressed in some of the primary Gnostic documents. The *Gnostic Gospel of Philip*, for example, states: "When Eve was still with Adam, death did not exist. When she was separated from him, death came into being. If he enters again and attains his former self, death will be no more."[15] That is to say, the physical male-female distinction (which arose in Eve's separation from Adam's side, as recounted in Genesis 2) is false and destructive; it is part of the fallen world of death, and we must escape it if we are to find true life.

The *Gospel of Philip* elaborates: "If the woman had not separated from the man, she should not die with the man. His separation became the beginning of death. Because of this, Christ came to repair the separation, which was from the beginning, and again unite the two, and to give life to those who died as a result of the separation, and unite them. But the woman is united to her husband in the bridal chamber. Indeed, those who have united in the bridal chamber will no longer be separated."[16]

The Gnostic *Gospel of Thomas* reiterates this message: "When you make the two one, and when you make the inside like the outside and the outside like the inside, and the above like the below, and when you make the male and the female one and the same, so that the male not be male nor the female female... then will you enter the kingdom."[17] The spiritual unification of the self, escaping the destructive biological definitions imposed by created gender, make up the soul's Gnostic salvation. Selfhood must not be defined by the false categories of male and female, invented by the evil Creator-God (not the true God) of Genesis.

Another Gnostic document, *The Exegesis on the Soul*, says concerning the soul: "As long as she was alone with the Father, she was virgin and in form androgynous. But when she fell down into a body and came to this life, then she fell into the hands of many robbers."[18] The implication is that it was the Fall that destroyed the original pure androgyny of the soul, rending the soul asunder into male and female "when she fell down into a body".

However, salvation is at hand. It is given through the soul's spiritual union with "the true bridegroom". And "once they unite with one another, they become a single life. Wherefore the prophet said concerning the first man and the first woman, 'They will become a single flesh.' For they were originally joined one to another when they were with the Father before the woman led astray the man, who is her brother. This marriage has brought them back together again."[19] The salvation of the soul restores her androgyny; the false biological markers of male and female are transcended in this Gnostic regaining of true identity.

We could spend considerable time investigating this theme of salvation according to Gnosticism, but enough has been said to show the essential idea. The Gnostic message is sufficiently plain. It declared war on the gender distinctions narrated in Genesis, dissociating human identity from the male-female norms expounded in the biblical creation account. Instead of this, Gnostics replaced the "biology of gender" with a completely disembodied and spiritualised notion of the human self, which transcended male and female, in favour of a subjectively defined self that was grounded in Gnostic mythology.

This view of the soul and its salvation meant, for example, that a Gnostic woman would achieve her true self by transcending the false category of her biological femaleness, and 'becoming male', in a spiritual sense: a type of 'liberation by choosing the opposite'. We encounter this in the *Gospel of Thomas*, where Mary Magdalene, through the Gnostic Jesus, has "become a male". In the *Gospel according to Mary Magdalene*, Mary likewise gives glory to the Gnostic Jesus thus: "Let us praise His greatness, for He has prepared us and made us into men".[20] The scholar of Gnosticism, Peter Jones, helpfully sums up this Gnostic theme:

> "The Gnostic Jesus teaches spiritual-sexual techniques of arousal, by which the disciple reaches states of mystical fusion with the All. In this state of out-of-body bliss, all distinctions, including gender distinctions, lose their power. Once reached, the state of ritual androgyny [androgyny acted out in rituals] then serves to underline the fundamental Gnostic conviction that redemption is liberation from all earthly and biological constraints."[21]

The analogy to modern transgenderism is very striking. We have now entered a cultural moment in which the Gnostic ideal has (under a different name) returned: the human self has been divorced from the constraints of its biology, so that it can define and redefine its gender subjectively, according to its own autonomous will. This separation of the definition of a person's self from his or her created biological sex is a theme held in common by ancient Gnosticism and modern (perhaps very secular) transgenderism.

Gnostics, of course, did not have access to modern transgender technology (hormonal treatments etc). But they had other ways of expressing physically their repudiation of the biological male-female distinction attested in early Genesis. They pursued this objective by attacking and subverting the pattern of human existence that arises from that male-female differentiation. Since, for Gnostics, the biological male-female distinction of early Genesis was false and destructive, they rejected the biblical channel for expressing the most intimate male-female relationship – sex within marriage. This epitomised all that Gnostics believed was wrong with this fallen creation. Many Gnostics therefore rejected sex altogether as something evil. Others took a different path, practising homosexuality, lesbianism, and sexual promiscuity.

A common motive, however, lay behind all these Gnostic repudiations of biblical sexual ethics – a fundamental rejection of the male-female biological 'binary' as definitional of human reality. The self had become fluid in Gnosticism, unbound from its physical and gendered trappings – not perhaps surprising, when we recollect that Gnostics regarded the entire world of matter, including physical flesh, as radically inferior (even alien) to the realm of spirit. The inner self alone had value; its fleshly vessel had no right to constrain or define it. For the Gnostic woman, therefore, this meant that marriage and motherhood became the supreme enemy. She redefined her biologically female selfhood by casting off its most obvious manifestations (being a wife, bearing children).

This ancient Gnostic outlook began to be reproduced in modern times, at first through the New Age movement. The New Age is relatively well-known for its feminine orientation: its opposition to 'patriarchy' (men exercising authority over women), and its embrace of a goddess-worshiping spirituality. Many of the leading female New Age thinkers are lesbians – not just as a matter of personal preference, but as a philosophical commitment. For example, Mary Daly, perhaps the foremost New Age feminist, openly admitted, "everything I write is an invitation to lesbianism".[22]

At root, however, this is all part and parcel of the ancient Gnostic ideal of androgyny: the idealisation of the human as transcending the body's biological categories of male and female. Since, normally, humans are either biologically male or female, the only way that androgyny can be approximated in practice is by homosexuality (men transcending their biological maleness by behaving as women), lesbianism (women transcending their biological femaleness by behaving as men), bisexuality, or most radically – for modern humanity – transgenderism (men seeking to transform themselves biologically into women, and women into men). The pattern is the same; transgenderism is its most cutting-edge form.

This anti-biological, androgynous ideal of gender has been graphically expressed in many modern New Age thinkers and writers. Actress and New Age populariser Shirley MacLaine, for example, on one of her inward mystical voyages into herself, saw "a powerful form, quietly standing in the centre of my inner space, looking at me with total love! The figure is very tall, an androgynous being with long arms and the kindest face... saying, 'I am the real you'."[23] According to MacLaine, the real you, the true human self, transcends gender. Our biology tells us nothing about who or what we are – in contrast to the biblical view that birth-gender is an aspect of the "real you". Mary Daly likewise explained: "What is at stake is a real leap in human evolution... [to] an intuition of human integrity or of androgynous being."[24] Another influential New Age mystic, Barbara Marx Hubbard, promises the readers of her book *The Revelation: A Message of Hope for the New Millennium*, that in the soon-approaching planetary awakening "you will be androgynous."[25]

In her book *Androgyny: Toward a New Theory of Sexuality*, June Singer, a modern Gnostic and psychologist of the school of Carl Jung (himself deeply sympathetic to Gnosticism and androgyny[26]), called for androgyny to be embraced as the new ideal of the human self: "We must look toward a whole way of being... no longer exclusively 'masculine' or 'feminine' but rather as whole beings in whom the opposite qualities are ever-present."[27] Singer even suggests that this should involve the creation of a new religion: "Can the human psyche realize its own creative potential through building its own cosmology and supplying it with its own gods?"[28]

Another significant promoter of Gnostic androgyny is the renowned expert on world religions, Mircea Eliade. Eliade argues that androgyny is the true, ultimate objective of religious mysticism: "in mystical love and at death, one completely integrates the spirit world; all contraries are collapsed. The distinctions between the sexes are erased; the two merge into an androgynous whole."[29] Eliade regards androgyny as "a symbolic restoration of 'Chaos', of the undifferentiated unity that preceded the Creation".[30]

Modern Gnosticism at this point joins hands with the revival of Paganism in today's Western culture, since neo-Paganism also has a marked affinity for the Gnostic view of the "true self". In the words of Lutheran theologian Carl Braaten, the newly revived Paganism embraces the view that "a divine spark or seed is innate in the individual human soul. Salvation consists of liberating the divine essence from all that prevents its true self-expression. The way of salvation is to turn inward and 'get in touch with oneself'."[31] This is precisely the path of the ancient and modern Gnostic, and it has obvious and immediate consequences for human identity: what if my true self that requires to be expressed contradicts my biological sex?

Sometimes the New Age Gnostic promotion of androgyny, and the transcendence of the self over biological norms, has seeped into the Church. For example, Episcopalian Matthew Fox, famous for advocating what he terms "creation spirituality", is an advocate of androgyny. His book *The Cosmic Christ* depicts on the cover a young naked Jesus of uncertain sex – is it a man or a woman? The message again is clear: the authentic self, represented by Jesus, is disconnected from gendered realities. The human psyche is beyond definition by biological maleness or femaleness. As if to underscore his rejection of Genesis gender norms, Fox also provocatively says, "In some ways homosexuality is superior to heterosexuality. There's no better birth control."[32]

Other indications of this encouragement of androgyny can be seen in the way the language of worship is being redefined. For example, a supplement to the hymnbook of the United Methodist Church in America has removed most masculine references to God. Just as the true human self is beyond biology, God is beyond all gendered references.[33] Along these lines, in some theology colleges in America that still define themselves as Evangelical, it is no longer acceptable to speak of God as Father; he must be called "Parent" to avoid any notion that gendered reference is appropriate or applicable to God. According to Genesis, humanity is made in God's image; when humanity redefines itself through Gnostic ideals that deny the boundaries of male-female biology, God inevitably ends up being remade in Gnostic humanity's image, purged of the masculine imagery of the Bible.[34]

And so we reach the perhaps surprising conclusion that the modern transgender movement, which allows people subjectively to define their own gender regardless of their biological maleness or femaleness, falls into the category of "nothing new under the sun". It is a modern re-statement of an ancient Gnostic belief. Once again, as in Gnosticism, the self has been detached from its fleshly embodiment, and allowed to redefine itself in a way that disowns the relevance of biological sex.

Ancient Gnostics had to rest content with carrying through this redefinition of 'true self' by (as we have seen) 'choosing the opposite' in terms of behaviour and lifestyle. The Gnostic woman showed that she was embracing androgyny, and rejecting the biological definition of her true self, by behaving as though she were a man (which explains the significance of Gnostic lesbianism). Modern transgenderism is able to take this a step further by employing modern medical techniques to remould female physiology, making it as much like a male as possible.

The kinship and parallelism of ideas, however, remain vivid. At the core of Gnosticism and transgenderism is the shared idea of the fluidity of the human self, unbounded by the maleness or femaleness with which it was 'encumbered' by its biology. The old Gnostic ideal of androgyny – that neither male nor female identity is determined by a person's physical characteristics given at birth, but that the true self transcends its biological sex – has received a new expression in today's climate. It is not necessarily as religious or spiritual as its Gnostic ancestor, but there is a commonality of ideas that must strike the Christian student of culture as profound and significant.

Conclusion

A Gnostic type of sexual ethics is filtering deeply into both the wider culture and the Church. Transgenderism fits into this pattern, displacing the human spirit (or self) from its fleshly embodiment, as ancient Gnosticism did, and modern New Age Gnosticism continues to do. Spirit/self then becomes free to define itself subjectively, untrammelled by the limitations of the flesh/biology. Of course, the ordinary 'person in the street' might maintain that this Gnostic or transgender outlook is correct, and the Genesis-grounded outlook of historic Christianity incorrect. What one cannot honestly do, however, is maintain that they are compatible or reconcilable.

Western society has arrived at a moment where it must choose between two alternative visions of human existence: either the embodied existence of the Genesis account of creation, with its acceptance of male and female biology as an aspect of our God-given selves, and its celebration of the human body (whether of man or woman) as fearfully and wonderfully made; or else the Gnostic rejection of the flesh and all biological norms, replaced by the celebration of a self-creating, self-defining self which aims at realising and fulfilling the spiritual autonomy suggested in the serpent's word to Adam and Eve – "You will be like God" (Genesis 3:5).

If we follow the Genesis account, we see that the serpent's promise was empty, and led to the loss of Eden and of immortality. Christians, at least, should know this, and therefore understand which path to follow and to commend. "Let your light shine before others, so that they may see your good works and give glory to your Father who is in heaven." (Matthew 5:16)

Appendix: The enduring significance of gender

There is a good argument from Scripture that gender – differentiation between male and female – endures on into the Resurrection. In other words, it will have an eternal significance for who we are. If so, this counts against the idea that gender is merely subjective and malleable. Rather, it is so woven into who men and women are, it will abide in the resurrection for eternity.

The main basis for believing in the enduring significance of gender is the biblical account of Jesus' own resurrection. The risen Lord was recognisably himself: there was continuity between his manifested identity in his state of humiliation (prior to and including his death) and his state of exaltation (post-resurrection). The resurrection did not transform him into some androgynous being, who could not be recognised as either male or female. He was still recognisably Jesus of Nazareth. The Gospel writers emphasise this by pointing out that he still bore the marks of his suffering: the nail prints in his hands, the wound in his side (although no longer experiencing pain from these). As if to say: behold Jesus, the very same Jesus known by the disciples before his death, now risen and glorified.

It is interesting in this respect that the risen Jesus still seems to have possessed his digestive organs. Luke records that the risen Lord ate fish and a honeycomb (Luke 24:41-43), in order to prove to the disciples that he was no ghost or spirit, but truly physically risen. This does not entail the conclusion that the risen Jesus would have died of starvation, without continual ingestions of fish and honeycomb or other edible earthly substances; after all, Paul says in 1 Corinthians 6:13, "'Food is meant for the stomach and the stomach for food'—and God will destroy both one and the other."

The ultimate life of resurrection in God's kingdom will not depend on edible food substances being ingested into a stomach. Yet in spite of no longer being dependent on physical food in his immortal and glorified body, the Lord evidently remained capable of eating – taking physical food into that body.

In Matthew's account of the Last Supper, the same point is made when Jesus says concerning the wine, "I will not drink again of this fruit of the vine until that day when I drink it new with you in my Father's kingdom". (Matthew 26:29). In the eternal kingdom, the glorified Jesus will, it seems, drink of the fruit of the vine. He will retain the capacity for drinking wine, although his possession of perfect immortality means that his body, now unable to die, will no longer be dependent for its ongoing life on such nutrition.

Some of the early Church Fathers were not slow in drawing the parallel here between digestive organs and sexual characteristics. If a resurrection body retains its capacity for eating and drinking, it seems likely (the fathers argued) that it also retains its characteristic maleness and femaleness. The analogy with eating and drinking, in other words, points in the direction of a *glorification* of the body's earthly characteristics, not their *abolition*. The very passage in 1 Corinthians 6 in which Paul states concerning food, "'Food is meant for the stomach and the stomach for food'—and God will destroy both one and the other", involves as its framework a discussion about the body's sexual activity in the life of the redeemed.

The parallel drawn by the fathers between the stomach and sex is therefore not forced, but totally natural in its context. If I, as a resurrected man, will retain my capacity to ingest physical substances (food and drink), the probability follows that I will also retain my maleness. My earthly characteristics are glorified, not abolished.

This teaching found among the early Church Fathers is summed up nicely by Jerome, translator of the Bible into Latin, and perhaps the greatest scholar among all the fathers. Referring to the resurrection, Jerome says: "The apostle Paul will still be Paul,

Mary will still be Mary".³⁵ Jerome's point is precisely the enduring significance of gender in the glorified life of the resurrection. Neither Paul nor Mary will lose their male or female characteristics. We will still recognise Paul as the *man* who preached Christ's unsearchable riches to the Gentiles (Ephesians 3:8), and Mary as the *woman* who was the "mother of my Lord" (Luke 1:43). Neither Paul nor Mary will become sexless or androgynous beings in the resurrection. The apostle Paul will still be Paul; Mary will still be Mary. Gender will be glorified, but not abolished.

Jerome's friend Augustine, the greatest theologian among the Latin Fathers, affirms the same:

> "For my part, they seem to be wiser who make no doubt that both sexes shall rise. For there shall be no lust, which is now the cause of confusion. For before they sinned, the man and the woman were naked, and were not ashamed. From those bodies, then, vice shall be withdrawn, while nature shall be preserved. And the sex of woman is not a vice, but her nature. It shall then indeed be superior to carnal intercourse and child-bearing; nevertheless, the female members shall remain adapted not to the old uses, but to a new beauty, which so far from provoking lust, now extinct, shall excite praise to the wisdom and clemency of God, who both made what was not and delivered from corruption what He had made".³⁶

Sometimes Jesus' statements about the non-existence of marriage in the world of the resurrection are taken as disproving the continued existence of maleness and femaleness. In Matthew 22:30 Jesus says, "in the resurrection they neither marry nor are given in marriage, but are like angels in heaven" (compare Mark 12:25). In Luke 20:34-36, he says, "The sons of this age marry and are given in marriage, but those who are considered worthy to attain to that age and to the resurrection from the dead neither marry nor are given in marriage, for they cannot die anymore, because they are equal to angels and are sons of God, being sons of the resurrection."

All that these statements disprove, however, is the existence of *marriage* (and sexual reproduction) in the resurrection. They say nothing about whether glorified gender will exist, along the lines proposed by Jerome and Augustine. Even though no longer "given in marriage", glorified Man will still be recognisably Man, and glorified Woman still recognisably Woman. Their distinctive forms will, as Augustine suggests, "remain adapted not to the old uses, but to a new beauty, which... shall excite praise to the wisdom and clemency of God". Paul will still be Paul, Mary will still be Mary, to the glory of the Creator and Redeemer of man and woman.

> *"All we who are human partake of the earthly nature of Adam. We are children of the dust. Our bodies suffer from all the weaknesses and frailties that belong to the earth. Our resurrected bodies will be tabernacles made in heaven. In the heavenly body, there will be no room for cancer or heart disease. The curse of the fall will be removed. We will be clothed after the image and likeness of the new Adam, the heavenly Man. Yes, there will still be continuity. We will still be men and women. Our personal identities will remain intact. We will be recognizable as the people we were in this lifetime. But there will also be discontinuity as the shackles of the dust will be broken by the heavenly form."*
>
> Sproul, R C, *Surprised by Suffering: The Role of Pain and Death in The Christian Life*, Ligonier Ministries, 2009, page 138

References

1. Lennon, J, *Skywriting by Word of Mouth*, Harper and Row, 1986, page 35
2. Paul makes the same point in 1 Corinthians 11:11-12 (ESV): "in the Lord woman is not independent of man nor man of woman; for as woman was made from man, so man is now born of woman." Man and woman, in their biological otherness, have a mutual interdependence. Woman, physically, came originally from Man (from Adam); but now, Man also comes from Woman (through childbirth).
3. The human race is called God's offspring in Paul's sermon on Mars Hill, Acts 17:28. This creational status of "offspring" differs from the redemptive adoption given in Christ.
4. Jesus quotes both Genesis 1:27 and Genesis 2:24.
5. Following Jesus' example, Paul quotes Genesis 2:24.
6. The original form of the Apostles' Creed reads:
   > I believe in God,
   > The Father Almighty,
   > Creator of heaven and earth.
   > And in Jesus Christ,
   > His only Son,
   > Our Lord,
   > Who was conceived by the Holy Spirit,
   > Born of the Virgin Mary,
   > Suffered under Pontius Pilate,
   > Was crucified,
   > Died and was buried.
   > On the third day He rose again.
   > He ascended into heaven
   > And is seated at the right hand of God the Father Almighty,
   > From where He will come again
   > To judge the living and the dead.
   > I believe in the Holy Spirit,
   > The holy Catholic Church,
   > The forgiveness of sins,
   > The resurrection of the dead,
   > And the life everlasting.

   Later, two other clauses were added: "He descended into Hades" (concerning Christ after His death), and "the communion of saints" (after "the holy Catholic Church").
7. For what follows, see Jones, P, *Spirit Wars*, Wine Press Publishing, 1997, chapters 10 and 11. *Spirit Wars* is one of the most comprehensive analyses and critiques of Gnosticism (ancient and modern) to have been written in recent times.
8. See Jones, P, *Spirit Wars*, Wine Press Publishing, 1997, page 145
9. From the message of Lazaris entitled *Concept: Synergy*, cited in *Ibid*, page 146
10. Alexander-Berghorn, K, 'Isis: The Goddess as Healer', in Nicholson, S (Ed.) *The Goddess Re-Awakening: The Feminine Principle Today*, Theosophical Publishing House, 1989, pages 96-97
11. Starhawk, M, *The Spiral Dance*, Harper and Row, 1979, page 193
12. From the RE-imagining Conference, Minneapolis 1993, as recorded in Ostrander, T, 'Who is Sophia?', *Priscilla Papers*, 8(2), 1994, page 2
13. Robinson, J, 'Very Goddess and Very

Man: Jesus' Better Self", in Davis S (Ed.) *Encountering Jesus: A Debate on Christology*, John Knox Press, 1988, chapter 4

14. This does not mean that all forms of Gnosticism necessarily, or explicitly, endorsed androgyny. But as Peter Jones, one of the foremost scholars of Gnostic thought, has shown in detail in his writings, androgyny was a powerful idea within the complex world of Gnosticism.
15. *The Gospel of Philip* (tr. Isenberg, W), see http://gnosis.org/naghamm/gop.html as at 8 November 2022
16. Loc cit
17. *The Gospel of Thomas* (tr. Lambdin, T), see http://www.gnosis.org/naghamm/gthlamb.html as at 8 November 2022
18. *The Exegesis on the Soul* (tr. Robinson Jnr, W), see http://gnosis.org/naghamm/exe.html as at 8 November 2022
19. Loc cit
20. *The Gospel of Mary*, see http://gnosis.org/library/marygosp.htm as at 8 November 2022
21. Jones, P, *Stolen Identity: The Conspiracy to Reinvent Jesus*, Victor: Kingsway Communications, 2006, page 101
22. Jones, P, *Spirit Wars, Op cit*, page 304
23. MacLaine, S, *Going Within: A Guide for Inner Transformation*, Bantam Books, 1989, page 87.
24. Cited in Jones, *Spirit Wars, Op cit*, page 189
25. Marx Hubbard, B, *The Revelation: A Message of Hope for the New Millennium*, Nataraj, 1995, page 165
26. For a useful account of Jung's Gnosticism and sympathy with androgyny, see Jones, P, Section IV: "The Religious Significance of Androgyny", Androgyny, *The Council on Biblical Manhood and Womanhood*, 1 September 1 2000, see https://cbmw.org/2000/09/01/androgyny/ as at 8 November 2022
27. Singer J, *Androgyny: Toward a New Theory of Sexuality*, Anchor Press, 1976, page 275
28. *Ibid*, page 124
29. Cave, D, *Mircea Eliade's Vision for a New Humanism*, Oxford University Press, 1993, page 154
30. Eliade, M, "Androgynes", in Eliade, M (Ed.) *The Encyclopedia of Religion*, page 277
31. Braaten, C E and Jenson, R (eds), *Either/Or: The Gospel or Neo-Paganism*, Grand Rapids, 1995, page 7
32. Steichen, D, *Ungodly Rage: The Hidden Face of Catholic Feminism*, Ignatius Press, 1991, page 230
33. *Washington Times Online*, 24 July 2001, see https://www.washingtontimes.com/news/2001/jul/24/20010724-024417-4398r/ as at 8 November 2022; *The Worldwide Faith News archive*, see https://web.archive.org/web/20091114100844/http://www.wfn.org/1999/05/msg00165.html as at 9 November 2022
34. Divine Fatherhood and Sonship are of course not biological, but human biological fatherhood is an earthly created image of God's Fatherhood within the Trinity. The apostle Paul says that all fatherhood is named after or according to "the Father of our Lord Jesus Christ" (Ephesians 3:14).
35. Jerome's Letter 75 (To Theodora), see https://www.newadvent.org/fathers/3001075.htm as at 14 November 2022.
36. Augustine of Hippo, 'The City of God XXII.XVII', in Schaff P (Ed.) *Nicene and Post-Nicene Fathers Volume 2*, Hendrickson, 2004, page 496.